STEALING SWEETS
AND PUNCHING PEOPLE

Phil Porter

STEALING SWEETS
AND PUNCHING PEOPLE

OBERON BOOKS
LONDON

First published in 2003 by Oberon Books Ltd.
(incorporating Absolute Classics)
521 Caledonian Road, London N7 9RH
Tel: 020 7607 3637 / Fax: 020 7607 3629

e-mail: oberon.books@btinternet.com
www.oberonbooks.com

A catalogue record for this book is available from the British
Library.

ISBN: 1 84002 404 6

Cover image: Ben Pacey

Printed in Great Britain by Antony Rowe Ltd, Chippenham.

Characters

EMILY
female, 16

MICK
Emily's dad, 42

MONICA
female, 46

BEN
male, 18

Stealing Sweets and Punching People was first performed at the Latchmere Theatre, London on 7 October 2003, with the following cast:

EMILY, Mariah Gale

MICK, James Duke

MONICA, Jacquetta May

BEN, Simon Bubb

Director, Crispin Bonham Carter

Set Designer, Philippa Kunisch

Sound Designer, Mike Winship

Lighting Designer, Andy Taylor

Production Manager, Phil Hewitt

Stage Manager, Nick Hayman-Joyce

for the Latchmere Theatre:

Artistic Director, Paul Higgins

Associate Director, Johnnie Lyne-Pirkis

ACT ONE

Scene 1

MICK and EMILY's bathroom. It is a Sunday evening in summer. EMILY is wearing a dressing gown and sitting on a chair. There are towels on the floor around the chair. MICK stands behind EMILY, cutting her hair.

EMILY: You're pinching my ear.

MICK: That's because you keep on moving.

EMILY: I keep on moving because you keep on pinching my ear.

MICK refers to a hairdressing book.

That book must be older than me. I don't know why you won't just let me go to the hairdressers. I'm pretty sure they wouldn't…strip me naked and tie me to the coat rack.

MICK resumes cutting.

Your hands smell like mandarin oranges.

EMILY sniffs the palm of her hand.

My hands smell like onions and chocolate. Hey look, it's like there's hair growing out of my hands. All the little clippings.

MICK: That's the first sign of madness.

EMILY: What is?

MICK: Looking for hair growing out of your hands.

EMILY: Is it?

MICK: That's what people say.

EMILY: Oh. Well I wasn't. I just noticed some clippings when I was sniffing my hand, that's all.

EMILY sniffs the back of her hand.

Do you ever think I might be going mad?

MICK: No.

EMILY: Seriously though. It's hardly exactly normal to dream about biting through glass bones.

MICK: You're not going mad.

EMILY: Seriously though.

MICK: I am being serious. Everyone has nightmares.

EMILY: You don't.

MICK: I have nightmares.

EMILY: What, dreaming you're trapped in a church full of birds? That's hardly as bad.

MICK: If you start wearing gloves on your feet, then we'll worry.

EMILY: I bet I wouldn't have nightmares if we still lived by the sea.

MICK: Don't be silly.

Pause.

EMILY: You'd better not be doing me another demented angel haircut.

MICK: You can look for yourself in a minute.

EMILY: That means you are. I wish you'd cut it short like the girl in the carpet shop. Long hair's itchy.

MICK: I don't want you looking like somebody else.

EMILY: Not likely when she's Chinese and twenty-two.

MICK: She doesn't look twenty-two.

EMILY: She is twenty-two. Anyway, what about me? I'll be sixteen in two weeks and a day. Please may I have…a smart black dress and a punnet of peaches? And a house by the sea.

MICK: Leave it, Emily.

EMILY: Do you remember when Mum tried to juggle with peaches? The little wet marks on the ceiling?

MICK: See what you think of that.

EMILY looks in the mirror and is disappointed. MICK gets down on all-fours.

These big old hands can be quite skilled when they want to be.

EMILY: Thanks Dad.

MICK: Now come and have a seat on the pony's back.

EMILY: That radiator's making funny noises.

MICK: It needs to be bled. Come on, come and sit on the pony's back.

EMILY sits on MICK's back.

I've been thinking… Do you think Monica would write me a reference?

EMILY: I didn't know you wanted a job.

MICK: Maybe.

EMILY: She might.

MICK: I'd still lay your clothes out and make your sandwiches.

EMILY: Don't be silly. I can do those things for myself.

Pause.

I know a certain thing about Monica, actually. I heard Monica talking about a certain thing, actually.

MICK: What's that then?

EMILY: Talking on the phone about a certain man.

MICK: Who's that then?

EMILY: She is so in love with you it's disgusting. I heard her on the phone to her sister last week, giggling like a complete idiot. She says your eyes are like sapphires or something. And your hands are so strong and gentle!

MICK: Is that what she said?

EMILY: It's exactly what she said. And when you speak to her she goes all hot and cold, she said. And she said she finds your shyness fascinating.

MICK: That's enough.

EMILY: And when she goes to bed she imagines you're her pillow.

EMILY stands up and moves away.

So what do you think of her? Do you imagine she's your pillow?

MICK: Of course I don't.

EMILY: That better not be a lie.

MICK: Honestly.

EMILY: So what then? Do you hate her?

MICK: No, I don't hate her.

EMILY: So you like her.

MICK: She's just all right. I like her like I like…

EMILY: What?

MICK: I don't know.

EMILY: The woman next door?

MICK: Yeah, like that.

EMILY: Or the dog next door.

Pause.

Which do you prefer? Monica or cheese and biscuits?

MICK: Don't be silly.

EMILY: I am deadly serious.

MICK: Cheese and biscuits.

EMILY: Monica or mouldy bread?

MICK: Monica.

EMILY: Monica or…the carpet on the landing?

MICK: I like them exactly the same.

EMILY gets back on MICK's back.

EMILY: Yeah well, that better be true is all I can say. I'd prefer for you to chop my fingers off than to fall in love with Monica.

MICK: Don't say things like that.

EMILY: I mean it. I'd never speak to either of you again. I'd prefer for you to stick lit matches up my fingernails –

MICK: Emily –

EMILY: I mean it. I need you to myself.

MICK: You've got me to yourself.

EMILY: I mean it. I'd kill you both. I'd die on my own.

MICK: That's all right. I need you too.

Short pause.

EMILY: All right.

Scene 2

MICK and EMILY's bathroom. It is about nine o'clock on a weekday morning and bright natural light shines into the room. MICK, wearing no shirt or socks, stands at the mirror and covers his face with shaving foam. EMILY comes in as MICK begins to shave. She is dressed smartly for work.

EMILY: Have you got butterflies?

MICK: I hardly slept five minutes.

EMILY: Don't worry, they'll definitely let you have it. Just as long as you don't sweat too much. And as long as your stomach doesn't make those dying dinosaur noises.

MICK takes a piece of paper from his pocket.

MICK: Ask me these.

EMILY: Do I have to?

MICK: Please. Settle my nerves.

EMILY takes the paper.

EMILY: Okay. Why do you want the job?

MICK: Okay. I've always had a genuine enthusiasm for coffee and catering and the serving of the general public. I'm a regular customer of the shop because I'm very keen on the pleasantness of the environment and the full-bodied flavour of the coffee that you serve. I would definitely relish the upkeep of your famous high standards. What do you think?

EMILY: You sound like a robot. What experience do you have on offer?

MICK: For several years I made hubcaps at a car plant and fitted them on by hand. Obviously, hubcaps aren't coffee, but nevertheless, I feel quite confident that I could transfer the skills that I have to your requirements.

EMILY: What would you do if a customer insulted you?

MICK: I would turn the other cheek.

EMILY: They won't ask you that. And what do you think of the uniform?

MICK: It's very nice. It's a very original colour.

Pause.

My stomach's like a shoelace in a knot.

EMILY: I'm running late for work.

MICK: Be careful when you're crossing roads.

EMILY: Okay. Don't forget to let the bath water out.

Pause.

MICK: Don't keep Monica waiting, love.

EMILY: I know, but only it's…

MICK: What?

EMILY: It's my birthday, Dad.

Short pause.

MICK: I am a complete idiot.

EMILY: It's no massive thing.

MICK: I am so sorry. So nervous, it slipped right out of my head. Happy birthday, Emily. I bought you what you wanted. It's underneath my bed.

He walks out.

(*Off.*) I'll make a cake this afternoon. I've got some candles somewhere.

EMILY: There's no need.

MICK comes back with a wrapped present.

MICK: Happy birthday, Emily.

She starts unwrapping it.

Just because the law says you're old enough to smoke –

EMILY: I would rather eat a lump of coal than smoke a cigarette.

EMILY holds up an old-fashioned, cream-coloured dress. She is sorely disappointed.

Thank you.

MICK: I looked at probably sixty different ones before I bought it. I bought it from a shop called Mrs Archibald's.

EMILY: It's really lovely material.

MICK: Good.

EMILY: And really beautiful…sewing.

MICK: Good. I didn't really know what size you were, but I showed her with my hands and she gave me this one. Anyway, if it doesn't fit, she'll swap it for another that does. Are you okay?

EMILY: I suppose.

MICK: I said you'd been quite late to develop. What's the matter?

EMILY: Nothing. Only I wanted a black one for smart occasions. And this one's really pretty and things, but it's kind of old-fashioned and kind of...babyish.

MICK: Emily, it's a present.

EMILY: The lace is totally gorgeous –

MICK: People aren't entitled to birthday presents. People just say thanks when they arrive.

EMILY: I did say thanks.

MICK: You didn't mean it very much.

EMILY: I did mean it.

Pause.

MICK: What smart occasions?

EMILY: There's a night at the school in October. We go back and get our certificates. If I wore this, people would laugh.

Pause.

MICK: I bought that dress on the day of the hailstorm. I trudged around for hours to find that dress.

EMILY: We can talk about it later.

MICK: I didn't realise I was buying a piece of rubbish.

EMILY: It's not a piece of rubbish. It's just a little bit strange.

MICK: There's nothing strange about it.

EMILY: It's a strange thing to buy me. It's a strange thing to wear. Especially now I'm sixteen. I'd look like a baby in a cream-coloured dress. I don't know why you always –

MICK: You're behaving like a baby.

EMILY: Dad –

MICK: Put it on.

EMILY: I haven't got time. I'm leaving for work.

MICK: Put it on and you can wear it to work.

EMILY: I'm not wearing that to work.

MICK: Put it on!

EMILY: Don't get upset with me.

MICK: I'm not upset, I'm angry with you and your rudeness!

MICK resumes shaving.

EMILY: Mrs Archibald's shop is a joke. The eyelashes on the mannequins have been stuck on upside down.

Pause.

You knew what I wanted. I wrote it with the letters on the fridge last week. 'Smart black dress,' I wrote. And I told you when you cut my hair, and I told you by the river.

MICK: I'd already bought it by then.

EMILY: You said you bought it on the hailstorm day. And what about my peaches? You do this all the flipping time, you never let me choose a thing, you bully!

MICK: Quiet now.

EMILY: You think that if you squash me then I'll always be a baby, but I won't. Everything changes whether you like it or not.

MICK: I said quiet now.

EMILY: You can't wrap me up in tissues. I'm a developing person!

MICK: I'm warning you.

EMILY: You wouldn't smack me.

MICK: I will in a minute.

EMILY: You're the one behaving stupid.

MICK: I will smack you in a minute!

EMILY: Whack me then! In the face! I'd rather that than wear your stupid dress!

EMILY throws the dress down. MICK drops his razor on the floor and moves towards EMILY. She covers her chest with her arms. He stands behind her. Putting one arm around her waist to control her, MICK tries to use his other arm to remove her shirt. She writhes and screams.

You're hurting me…

MICK: You're being spiteful and ungrateful –

EMILY: You're going to break my buttons!

MICK: And you think you know things that you don't. I'm ashamed of your behaviour.

EMILY: I'm ashamed of your behaviour!

MICK: Well, you're going to wear the dress –

EMILY: I don't want to wear the stinking dress –

MICK: You're going to wear the dress and you're going to walk to work in it.

EMILY: Dad, you're being weird! Dad! Just get off! Get off!!!

EMILY bites MICK's arm. MICK steps away. Pause.

You'll make me hate you if you act like that. Go and clean your shoes.

MICK leaves. After a moment, EMILY stoops to pick the razor up. The sound of the sea gently creeps into the room. When EMILY stands she sees someone in front of her. No actor plays this imaginary person.

I felt you there.

Pause.

Your eyes look like they're reading all the time.

EMILY squeezes the razor and drops it. Her hand bleeds.

I can feel my pulse in the blood.

EMILY walks to the bath with her bloody hand in front of her. The sound of the sea becomes louder and less gentle.

Look at my blood in the water, it's like red smoke.

EMILY feels her head being pushed towards the water.

No please. Please you're… Please, my neck. Your nails in my neck. Please I'm… Please…

EMILY's head goes under the water. She struggles. After a few seconds the pressure disappears. Her head comes up and the sound of the sea disappears.

Sorry sorry thank you thank you sorry completely thank you totally thank you sorry sorry thank you completely thank you completely thank you sorry sorry thank you.

Scene 3

MONICA's shop. The room is dusty and filled with antiques, junk, books and bric-a-brac. A large, sparsely filled, free standing unit of shelving holds some of the stuff. There is a box of new acquisitions on the counter. MONICA stands at the glass door, gazing out. EMILY is in the flat, which a door in the shop leads into. She cannot be seen.

MONICA: I always have a dream that my body turns to dust. Starting with my fingers and then up my arms and across my body, I crumble and get washed away by rain. Eventually I'm left with just my head on a yellow cushion.

EMILY: (*Off.*) I'd sooner dream that than biting through glass bones.

MONICA: Surrounded by candles and mice.

EMILY: (*Off.*) I'd sooner that than drowning with barbed wire round my legs. I'm scared to even shut my eyes.

MONICA: What does your Dad say about it?

EMILY comes in with a cup of tea and a gin and tonic. She has plasters on her hand. EMILY and MONICA begin tying labels round objects from the box and putting them onto the shelving unit.

What does your Dad say about your dreams?

EMILY: You know what he's like. He just stamps about and says I must be mental, then screams like mad and throws a load of ornaments at the wall.

MONICA: Since when did you have ornaments?

EMILY: You don't have to live with him. Honestly, some of the things he does, properly scary sometimes.

EMILY makes up a lie…

One time I didn't clean my shoes, so he tied my wrists to the bedpost.

MONICA: No he didn't.

EMILY: Yeah he did. Nine whole hours without even a cup of water.

MONICA: I'm sure that is a gross exaggeration.

EMILY: No smoke without fire.

Pause.

And he makes me ride him like a pony.

MONICA: What do you mean?

EMILY: He does, he makes me sit on his back like you'd sit on a pony, just to have a flipping conversation. I tell him I'm sixteen, but he just goes mad and threatens to kill me.

MONICA: Emily!

EMILY: It's the truth. Why are you taking his flipping side?

EMILY takes a mirror from the box and studies her face.

So much for the ugly duckling waking up as a beautiful swan.

MONICA: I don't know. A lot of girls would kill for bones like yours.

EMILY: Only a girl with no bones at all. My nose is identical to a white strawberry. My eyebrows are like a pair of hairy slugs on some kind of journey. If I had a face like the girl in the carpet shop –

MONICA: You'll be wishing for that skin back when you wake up flabby and dry and crumpled like me.

EMILY: I won't. I much prefer old faces. They remind me of things.

MONICA: Really? What does my face remind you of?

EMILY studies MONICA's face.

EMILY: It reminds me of…a half-collapsed house.

MONICA: Thank you so much.

EMILY: Or an underground cave or something. But I'd much rather that than have this greasy moon-face. It's not as if it pulls in crowds of boys.

MONICA: You can't expect boys to come flocking from nowhere and throw themselves at you.

EMILY: I wish they would.

MONICA: Sometimes you need to put yourself forward.

EMILY: But I do. I'm always thrusting myself forward. Okay, yesterday this nice-looking boy came in while you were out buying these. And he was flicking through the books and he had a silver flask, so I marched right up and asked him what was in it. But he just said soup. So I said 'Soup's not a meal,' because in my opinion it isn't, and he looked at me like I was covered in dog muck.

MONICA: Yeah. Maybe you put him on the spot a bit there.

EMILY: If he can't even cope with a girl like me –

MONICA: Or if you chose an easier subject like… television.

EMILY: There's a million things to say about soup.

MONICA: Or music. Or you could have asked him what he was looking for, or told him something interesting about something we sell. Or just asked a casual question like… 'Do you like the statue of the old man's head?'

EMILY: Do you like the statue of the old man's head?

MONICA: And told him it was carved by a one-handed sculptor.

EMILY: It was actually carved by a one-handed sculptor. He's not going to strip naked and jump on me because I go on about one-handed sculptors.

MONICA: No, but then you'd have a platform, wouldn't you. Once a conversation starts you have a platform to… I have no idea what I am talking about.

EMILY: Monica!

MONICA: With my track record, you should be teaching me.

EMILY: Monica, you were just getting interesting.

They continue their work.

MONICA: All I was going to say… Once you have a platform of conversation, then you have a chance to give off little signals. Don't you? You can use your body and operate in terms of body language. Reel in the fish.

EMILY: I don't know how to reel in the fish.

MONICA: Yes you do, follow your instincts.

EMILY: That's the problem. My instincts are as helpful as… nothing. The only thing that's natural to me is smiling like a wonky canoe. I need guidelines.

MONICA: You do not need guidelines from me.

EMILY: Yes I do.

MONICA: I am the last person.

They continue their work.

EMILY: Should I put my fingers up my nose? How do I reel in the fish, Monica?

MONICA: Just…little things.

EMILY: What little things?

MONICA: I don't know. Just the feminine things that women do to start to draw attention to their bodies.

EMILY: Which are?

MONICA: You might…play with your hair. Wind it into a spring around your finger. You know, like…

MONICA demonstrates the hair-winding technique. EMILY copies.

EMILY: I think he'd think I was a little bit demented.

EMILY experiments with the following techniques…

MONICA: Okay, you might stroke your neck or your wrists. Cross your legs at the top. And you might widen your eyes a bit. Look into his. Open your mouth a bit. Not quite as much as that. And you could tell him that he's interesting or looking good. Or lean across and touch him very slightly.

EMILY: With my hand?

MONICA: Just on the arm or the knee.

EMILY: (*Practising touching…*) What an interesting boy you are.

MONICA: And if you manage all of that and he's still not run away, then you're probably pretty much halfway there. Can you smell oranges?

Pause.

EMILY: Are those the tricks you try on my Dad, then?

MONICA: What do you mean?

EMILY: Or shouldn't I ask?

MONICA: I have never played tricks –

EMILY: Techniques then. Winding your hair in a spring and stroking your wrists. I'll keep my eyes peeled.

MONICA: Is that what you think?

EMILY: I'll tell him to watch out.

MONICA: I have never –

EMILY: Don't you dare, Monica. Don't you dare pretend you don't even like him because I heard the whole thing on the phone.

MONICA: You listen to me. I have absolutely no interest –

EMILY: You said you imagine he's your pillow! You said you had a dream where you were naked by a waterfall!

Pause.

MONICA: How dare you listen in.

EMILY: I wasn't.

MONICA: That is a private conversation.

EMILY: You were shouting your head off.

MONICA: I was not speaking about your Dad.

EMILY: What other Mick then? The only other Mick you know is the butcher. If you fancy a bloke with bits of raw bacon in his beard, you deserve to be shot.

Pause.

MONICA: You're being very stupid and very confused.

EMILY: I'm not being stupid.

EMILY puts an item on the shelf.

I'd sooner die than have my dad shifted away from me.

Scene 4

It is late afternoon in MONICA's shop and no-one is there. A takeaway milkshake is on the counter. MICK and MONICA enter together, carrying a large box. MICK wears the uniform of a coffee shop chain. MONICA's hair is tied up.

MICK: Who did you buy it from?

MONICA: Senile old woman. Husband just died.

They put the box down on the floor.

Cancer of the throat.

MICK: Oh right. Horrible.

They go back out and return with a slightly larger box.

MONICA: She called me a flesh-eating vulture. Said she could hear me beating my wings. Not very fair. Mind you, someone needed to beat their wings in that house. Ammonia like a wall.

They put the box down.

And hundreds of filthy little black dogs all yapping round my feet.

They go back out of the shop and come back with a heavy wooden chest.

I'm surprised that there's enough wind to fly a kite. You'd think the high buildings would act as a shield. Christ, this is heavy.

MICK: Just here?

MONICA nods. They put the chest down clumsily, jamming one of MICK's fingers between the chest and the floor.

Owww! Jesus owww!

MONICA: God, was that me? God, I'm sorry.

MICK: Flipping Christ!

MONICA: God, I'm sorry. Stupid butter fingers.

MICK: It's okay.

MONICA: I can't believe how stupid I am.

MICK: Really –

MONICA: Really, I'm so sorry.

MICK: Honestly, it's fine. Nothing broken.

MONICA: Let me see.

MICK: Just a bruise.

MONICA: God, I'm sorry.

MICK: Sorry. I didn't mean to shout like that.

Pause as MONICA inspects the finger.

MONICA: Bend your fingers.

MICK: There. Fine.

MONICA: It's starting to bleed there by the nail. Hold still, there's some plasters in the flat. Don't follow me, it's horrible in there.

MONICA goes into the flat. MICK opens one of the boxes with his uncrushed hand.

MICK: Look at that. There's even little waving people in little jumpers.

MONICA comes back with a plaster. Her hair is down.

MONICA: Found one. Hold out your hand.

MONICA puts the plaster on.

MICK: Thanks.

MONICA: There.

MICK: Thanks.

MONICA: Sorry.

Long pause.

Do you like the statue of the old man's head?

EMILY comes in, excited.

EMILY: Monica…! Oh, what are you doing here?

MICK: I brought you a milkshake. It's there on the counter.

EMILY: You're standing very close together.

MICK: She was putting a plaster on my finger. She dropped a heavy box on my finger –

EMILY: Who's she? The cat's mother?

EMILY takes a suck on her milkshake. MICK opens a box and pulls out some miniature train track.

MICK: Look at this, love. Old fashioned train set with all the bits. Monica bought it from some poor old woman –

EMILY: I know where she bought it. I work here, don't I?

MICK: Before our train set broke, we had these brilliant train set picnics, didn't we? Sending the sandwiches round in the carriages…

MONICA: You could buy this set.

EMILY: Who wants a sandwich off a load of mucky cancer carriages?

MICK: Emily –

EMILY: Who wants a train set picnic at all?

MICK: What's the matter with you?

EMILY: This milkshake's giving me a headache.

MICK: Then don't drink it so hard.

Sucking hard, EMILY goes to the door and looks out.

EMILY: Anyway, all I was going to say was that there's a boy in the park with a kite. He's standing on the old diving board.

MONICA: Oh really? What kind of kite?

EMILY: Don't ask me. Red and purple bird, it looks like.

MONICA: I'm surprised there's enough wind with all the high buildings.

EMILY: There's easily enough. Look if you don't believe me. He's flying it over the bandstand.

MONICA joins EMILY by the door.

He's been swooping it down on the pigeons. And making it dance round in circles and stuff.

MONICA: What a lovely thing.

EMILY: He tried to get this little girl to fly it, but she ran off with her hands in her pockets. Mmmm, white shorts and tanned legs…

MICK: I should get back.

EMILY: Not a moment too soon.

MONICA: That's not very nice. Thanks for the help.

MICK: Be careful when you're crossing roads.

EMILY: Why wouldn't I be?

MICK: Bye then.

MONICA: Bye.

MICK leaves. EMILY and MONICA watch the kite.

I was only putting a plaster on his finger.

EMILY: I wish I was whirling about in the sky. And not stuck down here with a stomach full of needles.

MONICA: Don't you feel well?

EMILY: That's not what I mean.

Pause.

I had an idea. I thought that if I caught a hundred pigeons. And tied them to a hundred bits of string. Then tied the bits of string to a set of clothes. Then put them on and banged a drum, all the pigeons would fly away scared and carry me up there with them. Carry me back to my house by the sea.

MONICA: You'd need to make sure they all flew in the same direction.

EMILY: That's the problem. They'd probably pull me up and up and then tear me apart in the sky. Imagine that, all my blood and bones.

Pause.

Monica, why do you sleep in here? Why do you hate your flat so much?

MONICA smiles and doesn't answer.

Still, at least you've got me. We have fun.

MONICA: We have fun.

EMILY: I like it when it's just you and me.

EMILY scratches her head.

My head's so flipping itchy today. It's worse than when I got sand in my knickers. Do you mind if I go and sit nearer the kite?

MONICA: I thought you liked having me all to yourself.

EMILY: But I want to see what he does with his hands.

MONICA: Okay.

EMILY leaves. MONICA moves to the boxes to unpack.

Scene 5

The park. BEN stands on a diving board above an empty old outdoor swimming pool, flying his kite. Steps lead up to the board. One of his shoelaces is untied. EMILY approaches quietly and stands a little way off. She watches his hands. He tugs on the rope and they watch the kite somersault. He does it again.

EMILY: Is that all it takes to make the kite somersault? Just a little tug on the string?

BEN: Yeah, when the wind's right.

EMILY: That's clever.

> *Pause.*

It's ever such a beautiful thing, isn't it? And you're really fantastic at flying it.

BEN: Thanks. It's only really a matter of practice.

EMILY: Monica was surprised that there's enough wind. All those high buildings and trees.

BEN: Yeah, the wind's not really blowing from that direction.

EMILY: That's what I said. Not that I know anything.

BEN: And this is quite an easy kite to fly. It doesn't really need too strong a breeze.

EMILY: Monica's my boss. My name's Emily.

BEN: Hi there. My name's Ben.

> *Pause. They watch the kite.*

EMILY: Actually, a band played in the bandstand until this year. Just on Wednesday evenings in the summer. But the conductor died in some kind of sleepwalking accident. The band's heart wasn't really in it after that. One of these benches is in loving memory of him. I don't know why you'd be interested in any of that, but I've said it now.

BEN: Would you like to fly the kite?

EMILY: No thank you.

BEN: Just for a moment. I need my hands to tie my shoelace.

EMILY: I'll tie your shoelace if you want.

BEN: There's no need for that. If you just hold onto the kite for a moment… I promise it's not very difficult. Come up.

EMILY: Okay.

EMILY joins BEN on the diving board.

BEN: Okay, hold out your hands.

EMILY holds out her hands with trepidation. BEN puts the kite into EMILY's hands, also keeping hold himself.

My goodness, your hands are on fire. Are you ready for me to let go?

EMILY: I think so.

BEN: It pulls a bit harder than you probably think.

EMILY: Maybe I shouldn't –

BEN: But as long as you keep your hands down by your body and your fingers quite tight round the handle… That's it. You'll be fine. Three. Two. One.

Slowly, BEN takes his hands from around EMILY's. EMILY is thrilled. BEN bends down and ties his shoelace.

How does that feel?

EMILY: Lovely. Really lovely.

Pause.

It's like some kind of animal, the way it jerks about. It's like a dog on a lead in the sky. Have you ever been blown off your feet?

BEN: Not that I remember.

EMILY: It makes me feel quite fluttery myself.

Pause.

Do you think that there was ever any water in the swimming pool?

BEN: I suppose there must have been once.

EMILY: What a stupid question. Looks horrible with all that broken glass and flaky paint.

Pause.

BEN: Look at that. Your knuckles are white.

EMILY: That's because I need to be careful not to let go. My fingers have brains of their own sometimes. Like if I hold a teacup, my fingers sometimes decide to drop it without even asking me first. Just a sudden rush of blood to the fingers. And I work in an antique shop, so it's hardly ideal.

BEN: I can imagine.

EMILY: Halfway between antiques and junk really. Nobody ever comes in.

BEN: I'm exactly the same with eggs. If I hold one in my hand, I can't help crushing it.

EMILY: Really?

BEN: Yeah, absolutely. The more I try to hold it gently, the stronger the temptation is to squeeze.

EMILY: That's exactly like me and the bat.

BEN: What bat's that?

EMILY: Oh, it wasn't anything really. I found a bat with a broken wing and looked after it until it was better. But when I picked it up to let it go, I squeezed too hard and it broke again.

Short pause.

I don't know why I'm telling you things like that. I'll make you think I'm mental.

BEN: You're flying it like you've been flying kites all your life.

EMILY: I wish I had been. Do you want it back now?

BEN: No thanks. I'll watch you and pick up some tips.

EMILY: Watch me? Don't be ridiculous. It'll probably nosedive and plonk on the bandstand roof in a minute. I'm just amazed that it stays in the sky at all.

BEN: It hardly weighs anything really. It's just a few sticks of wood with some Japanese silk stretched across.

EMILY: Japanese silk?

BEN: And then with the aerodynamics…

EMILY: How much did it cost? I bet I can't afford one.

BEN: Oh, I didn't actually buy this one, I made it. The materials cost a little bit but –

EMILY: You're joking. You actually made it?

BEN: Yeah, it's much more fun if you make your own.

EMILY: But it's beautiful. The shape of it and the colours are just so –

BEN: Obviously, I bought the silk.

EMILY: But it's beautiful. If I could make something as beautiful as that…

BEN: It's honestly just a few sticks and some silk. I could show you some time if you wanted.

EMILY: Really?

BEN: Of course. I could teach you to make all sorts if you wanted. Box kites, man-lifters, dragon kites, all of that. I learnt it all off my Dad, you see. He used to sit at the kitchen table and –

EMILY: Is he dead now?

BEN: Who?

EMILY: Your Dad.

BEN: No, he's still alive.

EMILY: Sorry. I'll shut my mouth.

BEN: Why did you ask that?

EMILY: Sorry. What a stupid thing to say.

BEN: I'm just curious –

EMILY: My mouth, it's like my fingers. It's like a stupid runaway train. I'd better go back.

BEN: No, stay.

EMILY: Take the kite back.

BEN: No honestly, I'm not offended, I'm just curious. Because it's funny you should ask. Because in some ways he might as well be…dead, in a way. I mean, I never really see him any more.

EMILY: Oh.

BEN: He left my Mum for another woman a couple of years ago. Moved abroad and we haven't spoken since. I just thought perhaps you'd picked up on that. You seem like perhaps the sort of person that might.

EMILY: Really?

BEN: Yeah. You seem…like the sort of person that might.

EMILY: Oh. I don't know if I did or I didn't.

BEN: He's a hairdresser.

Pause.

EMILY: I wish my Dad would pay a bit less interest. Sorry, I didn't mean that.

BEN: It's okay.

EMILY: I just mean he's quite suffocating. I think his biggest wish would be to freeze me as a ten-year-old. But the more he wraps me up in tissue, the more I feel like breaking free. I love him more than anything but… Can you take the kite now? I need to scratch my head.

BEN takes the kite. EMILY scratches her head, then begins to wind her hair around her finger.

Even though it's sticks and silk, it must be heavier than air.

BEN: The kite?

EMILY: Yeah. So why does it float?

BEN: Oh, that's just a matter of aerodynamics really. The air that passes across the upper side travels faster than the air beneath, so the change in the air pressure pushes it upwards.

EMILY: That's clever.

BEN: There's more air underneath, so the kite gets pushed up higher. It's exactly the same with aeroplanes, but they're quite a lot heavier.

EMILY: (*Touching BEN.*) Yeah. What an interesting thing.

BEN: Have you ever seen the magic paper trick? That's just a matter of aerodynamics.

EMILY: I don't think I have.

BEN: It's not really magic, it's just a matter of science. It's probably quite boring –

EMILY: Show me it.

BEN: Are you sure?

EMILY nods.

Okay, have you got a bit of paper? Just a little bit of paper?

EMILY: I don't think I have.

EMILY feels in her pocket and takes out a shopping list.

Yes I have, I've got a shopping list. Well, it's not really a list. It just says margarine.

BEN: That's perfect. Okay, tear a little slit just in the middle of it.

EMILY tears a slit.

EMILY: I've done that.

BEN: And give it to me.

EMILY gives the paper to BEN, who pushes the handle of the kite through the hole in the paper, so that it sits at the bottom of the string.

Now, gently put your hands around the paper. Just like you'd put your hands around a grasshopper.

EMILY puts her hands around the paper. BEN puts one hand on top.

Close your eyes and make a wish.

EMILY closes her eyes.

Your hands are shaking.

EMILY: My whole body's shaking for some reason.

BEN: Have you made a wish?

EMILY nods.

Then very slowly, open your eyes and move your hands away and watch the piece of paper.

EMILY does this. The piece of paper quickly dances up the string and out of sight.

EMILY: That's amazing!

BEN: I love it –

EMILY: It's the best thing in the world! How did you do that?!

BEN: Exactly the same principle. The air underneath –

EMILY: It knows exactly where it wants to go! You do one and I'll hold the kite. I've got a big receipt from the margarine.

EMILY pulls a receipt from her pocket. She tears a slit in it and gives it to BEN, who puts it on the string.

I don't think I've ever seen anything better! It's like a little dance or something! Hold onto the paper and I'll take the handle.

EMILY takes the handle from BEN. He cups the receipt.

And close your eyes and make a wish.

BEN closes his eyes.

BEN: I wish –

EMILY: Don't tell me! If you say it out loud then it won't come true.

BEN: Okay.

Pause.

EMILY: Tell me. Tell me what you're wishing for.

BEN opens his eyes and smiles at EMILY. He lets go of the paper and it dances up the string.

Scene 6

MICK and EMILY's bathroom. It is early evening. The room is lit warmly and the window is open. EMILY comes in, wearing her work clothes and carrying a white blouse, a black skirt, some tights, a bowl of salad and a fork. She presses play on a CD player and some music begins to play. She takes off her clothes, except for some black underwear, sprays two sprays of perfume into the air and stands in the perfumed area. She puts the chair in front of the mirror and sits on it. She eats a forkful of salad and watches herself brushing her hair. She has a couple of small bruises and scabs on her body. MICK comes in and switches off the CD player.

MICK: Why are you eating salad? You said you were going to a restaurant.

EMILY: I said we might eat in a restaurant. We haven't made fixed plans. Anyway, it's only a few bits of lettuce.

MICK: The perfume in here, I'm amazed you can swallow –

EMILY: I only did two sprays and we're not meeting for another hour.

Short pause.

MICK: I'll probably put something in the microwave.

EMILY: Will you do my make-up, Dad? When I do it myself I come out like a snowball. Either that or a satsuma.

38

MICK: Not tonight.

EMILY: Seriously though. I was thinking you could do my eyes like you did mine and Mum's at Christmas times. Slightly Chinese.

MICK: I can't remember –

EMILY: Yes you can, and our cheeks all perfect.

MICK: I can't.

Beat.

EMILY: Please though –

MICK: I said already!

EMILY: There's no need to be so weird about it.

EMILY sprays her neck with perfume.

Have you seen my butterfly hair clip? It was so funny this morning. I watched this injured butterfly walk round and round in perfect circles until...

EMILY stands and turns to face MICK.

Have you seen my butterfly hair clip?

MICK: That's new underwear.

EMILY: This? Yeah, do you like it? I bought it at lunchtime. The woman in the shop said it made me look quite elegant.

MICK: You said you read a book at lunchtime.

EMILY: Yeah, when I got back. Anyway, you'd better like it because I tried on about sixty different kinds. Blue, green, cherry, flowers, purple. They even had bras with strings that you pull. The woman in the shop had the perfect body. Men would see her and explode. What?

MICK: You shouldn't keep secrets.

EMILY: What's the secret? You're staring at them now, aren't you?

MICK: I could have helped you buy them.

EMILY: I didn't need your help. When did you become an expert on women's underwear? Or shouldn't I ask?

Short pause.

Anyway, I've bought them now, so what do you think? The woman in the shop said they make me look quite elegant. What do you think?

MICK: Think about what?

EMILY: Do they make me look quite elegant or not?

MICK: I don't know. Look in the mirror.

EMILY: Why don't you like them?

EMILY looks in the mirror. Pause.

What's the matter? Is it the colour? Is it because they're not white?

MICK: No.

EMILY: Because I know what you think about black, but they didn't have any in white. Obviously, they had some in white…

EMILY poses in the mirror.

Do you think they don't fit me right? Because I feel like I'm bursting out, but she said I needed boosting. Probably right really.

MICK: They're fine.

EMILY: Then what then?

MICK: What?

EMILY: Why are you acting as if the sky just collapsed?

Pause.

That radiator's still making funny noises.

MICK: It needs to be bled.

EMILY: Then bleed it then.

MICK: How much did they cost?

EMILY: Is this all about stupid money?

MICK: I'm just asking how much. Tell me how much.

EMILY: You're like a boring calculator.

MICK: Just tell me how much.

Short pause.

EMILY: A bit more than fifteen pounds if you must know.

MICK: How much more than fifteen pounds?

EMILY: About fifteen pounds more, but it's my money.

MICK: Thirty quid! You're saving for a bike!

EMILY: I don't want a bike, I want this.

MICK: You can't afford both!

EMILY: I don't want both!

MICK: Well they won't get you to work!

EMILY: Well I can't wear a bike! I'm too flipping old for Mickey Mouse crop-tops. The woman giggled when she saw. You always tell me how to spend my money.

MICK: It's not the money.

EMILY: It's me that does the hours.

MICK: I said it's not the money!

41

EMILY: I know it's not the money! You think I bought them for tonight!

MICK: Of course you bought them for tonight.

EMILY: You think I'm going to strip right off the moment that I see him. We all wear underwear, it doesn't mean we show it. It doesn't mean we just open our legs!

MICK: When you spend thirty pounds –

EMILY begins to put on the white blouse.

EMILY: I think I'll wear some other clothes as well, come to think of it.

MICK: Don't be funny.

EMILY: What's funny?

MICK: I know exactly what you're like.

EMILY: Then you know that I'm not some stupid dirty idiot!

Pause. EMILY puts on the tights.

MICK: Everyone has feelings and everyone gets excited –

EMILY: Are you some kind of vicar?

MICK: I am trying to stop a mistake being made.

EMILY: Really? Well, thanks and everything but we were planning to do it up against a cathedral at sunset.

MICK: You stop that –

EMILY: And then we thought we'd do it in a toilet!

MICK: Stop that right now.

EMILY: What do you think I am Dad?

MICK: When you spend your wages on things like that –

EMILY: It makes me feel good! It's not dirty. It makes me feel less like a scruffy little clumsy little girl.

Long pause. MICK gets down on all-fours.

MICK: Come on.

EMILY: No.

MICK: Come and have a seat on the pony's back.

EMILY: Don't you understand anything? I'm a developing person. I don't need stupid games –

MICK: Sit on the pony's back and we'll talk about it.

EMILY: I won't sit on the pony's back. I'm not some kind of –

MICK: Sit on the pony's back.

EMILY: I won't. I'm not some kind of –

MICK: Sit on the pony's back.

EMILY: I won't! I'm trying to tell you something!

Pause.

I'm not some kind of doll in a glass box, all right? I'm not just a thing for you to squash, all right?

The phone begins to ring in another room.

Answer the phone.

Short pause.

Answer the phone.

MICK: Will you please just come and sit on the pony's back?

EMILY: It's your fucking back, Dad, and I'm not fucking sitting on it!

MICK grabs EMILY and begins to shake her.

MICK: Don't you ever…

EMILY: Please Dad please!

MICK: Ever speak like that to me!

EMILY: I didn't mean it.

MICK: Ungrateful…

EMILY: I didn't mean it.

MICK: Don't you ever speak like that to me!

EMILY: Stop it, Dad! Stop shaking me!

He stops. They stand frozen. Pause.

Stop shaking me. I was just trying to tell you something. Just that you… chain me up too much.

Pause.

Answer the phone. It hardly ever rings.

MICK leaves the room. EMILY picks up a tissue and dabs her eyes. The sound of the sea creeps into the room. EMILY turns around.

Would you like to touch my clothes?

EMILY lies down on the floor. She laughs as if in pain. She stands up. Pause.

Would you like some salad? My stomach's like a bag of nails.

EMILY takes a forkful of salad and holds it out in front of her.

Open your mouth.

EMILY's hand closes tight around the fork handle, its prongs pointing downwards. The sound of the sea increases.

Please Mum, you're crushing my hand. Please let go.

EMILY stabs the fork into her own leg. She screams. Beat.

Please you mustn't –

She stabs again. Beat.

No Mum.

Again.

No please no –

Again.

Please don't.

Again.

My leg! Stop Mum!

Again.

Stop!

Again.

Stop Mum!

Again.

Please stop! There'll be blood!

Twice more.

Mum, there'll be blood!

As she continues to stab.

You mustn't you mustn't you mustn't you mustn't you… Please!!

EMILY throws the fork across the floor. The sound of the sea disappears.

Thank you thank you absolutely sorry completely sorry sorry thank you completely thank you so much sorry so much sorry so so so so sorry…

MICK comes back.

…Sorry sorry sorry…

MICK: Emily?

EMILY: Sorry sorry sorry sorry completely sorry sorry. Completely sorry.

MICK kneels behind EMILY and holds her.

MICK: There you go, can you feel my arms around you there?

EMILY: Yeah.

MICK: Can you feel me looking after you there?

EMILY: Yeah.

MICK: No need for any of this.

MICK gently strokes parts of EMILY's head as he speaks.

That's me stroking your eyebrows. Little silver button nose. Mouth. Hot cheeks. Come on, let me clean this pretty face.

EMILY sits on the chair and MICK kneels in front of her. He puts cleanser on a cotton wool pad and wipes her face.

So fragile, look at you. Tied together with thread.

He cleanses her face in silence for a while.

Feeling better?

EMILY: Yeah.

MICK: Close your eyes.

MICK cleanses her eyelids…

Never mind, we can play a board game instead.

EMILY: What?

MICK: More fun than a restaurant any day of the week.

EMILY: Dad, please let me go.

MICK: Look at you, you're in no state to go out.

EMILY: Please, I didn't mean to speak like that.

MICK looks in her hair.

I was joking about the cathedral, he will not touch me –

MICK: Emily, your hair!

Beat.

EMILY: My hair?

MICK: It's crawling with lice. It's like a nest.

EMILY: Don't tell lies.

MICK: There's one on my hand.

EMILY: Stop it.

MICK: Look, there's two on my hand.

EMILY: (*Pushing hand away.*) Stop lying to me.

MICK pushes EMILY towards the mirror and holds her hair to create a parting…

MICK: Look for yourself.

EMILY: I can't see anything.

MICK: There on your scalp. Eggs.

EMILY: I know what you're doing. You're pathetic, you're mean is what you are.

MICK: You don't mean that.

EMILY: I hate you for this. You can't stop me going.

MICK: Stay here, I'll wash your hair –

EMILY: It doesn't need washing!

MICK: You'll infect him, you don't want that.

EMILY: There's nothing there, you liar! You liar, it's got nothing to do with my hair! It's you! You're weird! Stuff you, I'm going.

MICK: (*Grabbing at EMILY as she stands.*) Emily –

EMILY: (*Fighting free.*) Get off me!!!

MICK: You sit back down.

EMILY: Don't wait up.

MICK: Sit down.

EMILY: Cheerio.

MICK: I said sit down I will not let you go!!! I will not let you go!!!

EMILY freezes with her hand on the door handle.

I am telling you… I will punish you…

EMILY: No you won't.

MICK: If you go I will, I'll punish you.

EMILY: I don't care.

EMILY opens the door. MICK runs across and grabs her by the waist. He tries to hoist her away from the door. She screams, clinging to the handle. She lets go and flies across the room, landing in a heap.

MICK: You need to be here!

Long pause.

EMILY: Daddy…

MICK: You need to be here with me.

EMILY: Please… Daddy…

MICK takes the key from the door, leaves the room and locks the door from the outside. EMILY walks to the door and tries to open it. She sits for a moment, then notices the open window. She sticks her head out of it and looks down.

ACT TWO

Scene 1

The park. It is a warm evening. BEN stands on the grass by the diving board steps, scruffily dressed, waiting for EMILY. He looks into a plastic bag of things that he is carrying. He checks his watch. EMILY arrives, dressed as before but with a rip in her skirt.

EMILY: Ben?

BEN: Hi there. I thought you'd had a change of heart.

EMILY: Sorry. Something stupid held me up.

BEN: I was thinking I'd got the wrong day. My goodness, what perfume.

EMILY: Do you like it?

BEN: Yeah.

EMILY: It reminds me of Spain. Not that I've actually ever been.

    Short pause.

BEN: You never told me you were a waitress.

EMILY: I beg your pardon.

BEN: You never told me… Are you a waitress? I just assumed you were a waitress because of the… Are you a waitress?

EMILY: No, I work in an antique shop.

BEN: Sorry, just the clothes. Not that there's anything –

EMILY: These are my clothes for tonight. Actually, I just wore them as a joke. I thought that it might make you laugh if I dressed like a waitress.

BEN: Oh. Very good. And anyway, it suits you.

Short pause. BEN puts his bag on the ground, kneels beside it and begins to take sticks from it.

I thought we could start with a man-lifter. What do you think? It's just three strong sticks on a hexagon really, but you get tremendous lift.

EMILY: I don't know what you mean.

BEN: I mean it lifts into the air very easily. The ground's a bit wet. We could go back up on the diving board. Why are you looking like that?

EMILY: I thought that we were going to a restaurant or something.

BEN: Restaurant? Why? I mean, I've eaten. I mean, I thought you wanted teaching about kites.

EMILY: Not right now.

Short pause.

BEN: I brought some old diagrams –

EMILY: But you said. You said the city lights inspired your poems. And I said let's meet up on Friday night.

BEN: I did say that, but I thought you were referring to that earlier moment. When you'd said…

Short pause.

Forget it. Let's go into town.

EMILY: Really?

BEN: Yeah, let's go into town.

EMILY: We could go for a drink if you've not left any room.

BEN: You're only just sixteen.

EMILY: I don't care. Monica lets me taste her gin.

BEN: There's a rip in your skirt.

EMILY: Yeah, I caught it on a nail.

Short pause.

BEN: Okay, we'll go for a drink. What time do you need to be home?

EMILY: No particular time. My Dad's quite laid back.

Scene 2

It is early night-time in MONICA's shop and the room is lit by a lantern or lamp that is for sale. She has laid the train set out on the floor in a circle. She sits on the floor in the centre of the circle with a remote control, a bottle of gin, a bottle of tonic and a packet of straws. The goods train travels round and round. She stops it in front of her, pours gin into one truck and tonic into another. She sucks some gin up with a straw, then sucks some tonic up. She is mixing them in her mouth when there is a loud bang at the door. She starts to tidy the bottles away.

MONICA: Wait a minute. I won't be a minute.

Another loud bang. MONICA leaves the bottles and opens the door.

All right, no need to break the door. Mick, what a surprise! I was just… Would you like to come in?

MICK comes in and MONICA rushes back to tidy the bottle and straws away. MICK is very wet. He carries a bottle of wine.

I thought you were an axe murderer, the way you were banging. I'm sorry it's such a mess in here. I'm sorry it's so dark in here.

MICK: I was passing by. I thought your ankle had twisted.

MONICA: My ankle?

MICK: I saw you through a crack in the curtains. I saw you on the floor.

MONICA: No, my ankle's fine. I should draw the curtains better, I was just… Jesus Christ, you're soaking wet.

MICK: Yeah, I got caught. In a shower.

MONICA: My God, shall I hang your coat up?

MICK gives MONICA his coat and she hangs it up…

It must have been hammering down. I might as well be blind and deaf, I'm so oblivious to the world sometimes.

Pause.

There, nothing worse than wet clothes.

Pause.

You're very still and quiet. Did you want anything in particular or… It's lovely to see you –

MICK: I bought you a bottle of wine.

MONICA: That's for me?

MICK: I bought it to apologise.

MONICA: Oh you needn't have bothered. Sorry, apologise for what?

MICK: I bought it to apologise for shouting like that. You dropped that box on my finger…

MONICA: That's very kind. I did drop a box on your finger.

MICK: Yeah well… I've bought it now.

MICK gives MONICA the bottle. Short pause.

MONICA: Is something the matter? You seem anxious. Is there anything the matter?

MICK: No. Nothing.

MONICA: Would you like to sit down?

MICK: You look very beautiful.

MONICA: Thank you, I'm… Thank you, I don't know what to say.

Pause.

I think I might carry on dusting. Do you mind if I carry on dusting? You know what dusting's like…

MONICA dusts frantically…

So I bet she looked wonderful didn't she, leaving the house? I thought she was going to combust this afternoon. She sat on the floor there learning famous quotations, biting her nails down to her knuckles. I said 'What do you plan to do, just slip them in?' Well she said she did, so I dread to think. What shoes did she wear?

MICK: I don't know.

MONICA: She was torn between laces and buckles.

MICK: Yeah buckles.

MONICA: And what about her hair in the end?

MICK: I don't know.

MONICA: She said she might tie it up but she's got such beautiful hair –

MICK: I don't know. I didn't see.

MONICA: Yes, well, anyway, what could go wrong in that new underwear?

MICK: What do you mean?

MONICA: Nothing. Sorry. I'm feeling slightly giddy, I don't know why. Shut up Monica.

MONICA continues her dusting in silence. MICK lays his hand on the centre of MONICA's back and she stops.

MICK: Can we drink the wine now?

MONICA: Drink it now? I shouldn't really –

MICK: I thought we could drink it now.

MONICA: Okay. Okay, let's drink it now. Celebrate… everything. You open it, I'm feeling slightly…

MONICA gives MICK a corkscrew. He opens the bottle.

Do you want to know what I was really doing on the floor?

MICK: What were you doing?

MONICA: You'll think I'm stupid… I couldn't lay my hands on a glass, that's all. I couldn't lay my hands on a glass so I was sucking up gin from the goods train instead. Now look me in the eye and tell me I'm not a lunatic.

MICK: Yeah, I saw you through the curtains.

MONICA: Oh. Well you shouldn't be surprised, I'm sure she's told you I drink gin and tonic from a gravy boat.

MICK: No, she never told me that.

Pause. The cork comes out.

MONICA: I'll fetch some glasses. I'd invite you through, but it's horrible –

MICK: We could drink it from the train.

MONICA: Very funny –

MICK: Let's drink it from the train.

MONICA: I am capable of drinking from a glass.

MICK: I want to drink from the train.

Beat.

MONICA: Okay. I don't know when I last swept the floor.

MICK and MONICA kneel by the track.

Is it very hot in here?

MICK: (*Wiping his head…*) No, that's just raindrops.

MONICA: Okay, but if you want me to open a window…

MONICA pours wine into a truck and gives MICK a straw.

We must look very…

MICK drinks.

Yes and while she was memorising quotations, I was fixing this thing together. Which was not easy at all.

MICK puts his hand on MONICA's leg.

Kneeling on sharp bits of…sharp bits of plastic.

Pause. MICK kisses MONICA.

I'm so happy.

MICK: Good. That's good.

MONICA: I've wanted this so much. You have no idea…

MICK: That's good then.

MONICA: I've been so lonely.

Pause. They kiss again.

I'm so pleased. I had no idea.

MICK: Yeah.

MONICA: I had no idea you felt like this.

MICK: I need you.

MONICA: I'm so pleased.

MICK: Yeah, I really need you.

They kiss again. Pause.

MONICA: Would you like some more wine?

MICK: Yes please.

MONICA: In the name of celebration.

MONICA pours some wine into a truck. MICK drinks.

You look like an anteater sucking up ants.

MONICA giggles.

I feel like a schoolgirl. I'm so excited, I feel fourteen. I feel like dancing in the street. How do you feel?

MICK: Really pleased.

MONICA: The time I've spent wishing... I suppose I have Emily to thank for this sudden display of affection.

MICK: What do you mean?

MONICA: I don't know, her being out there now, this sudden burst of romance in her life... I guess that must have helped these feelings come to light.

MICK: In what way would it do that?

MONICA: I don't know really. I suppose the idea that she's reaching that stage in life might make you feel a bit... lonely? I feel lonely all the time. I don't know, does it make you feel lonely?

MICK: She's only gone out for one night.

MONICA: Yes, but as she grows up…

MICK: It's nothing to do with loneliness.

MONICA: Okay, not loneliness then but…

Short pause.

MICK: Not loneliness but what?

MONICA: I don't know, maybe just the tiniest hint of jealousy?

MICK: Jealousy?

MONICA: You know.

MICK: I don't think I'm jealous.

MONICA: Sorry –

MICK: Why would I be jealous of my own daughter?

MONICA: Oh no, not jealous of Emily, jealous of Ben. I mean that you might be slightly jealous of him.

MICK: Why would I be jealous of him?

MONICA: Well because… It really doesn't matter. I have no idea what I'm talking about. Let's not spoil things. There are so many other things to talk about.

Pause.

I'm certainly not suggesting anything unusual, anything unnatural. I know nothing about it, so I should keep quiet, but I don't think it's at all uncommon for a father to feel…for a father to struggle to come to terms with his daughter's development, sexual development. I'm certainly not accusing you of…anything.

Short pause.

But you must admit that you have quite a strange relationship.

MICK: We don't find it strange.

MONICA: I don't mean strange, I mean intense.

MICK: I don't see what's so intense.

MONICA: Please don't be offended.

MICK: I'm not offended, I don't see what's so intense.

MONICA: I don't think it's a bad thing. I don't know, I only go on what I hear, but I'd say it's quite intense. I'd say it's probably…not a very normal relationship. But define normal –

MICK: Has she said something?

MONICA: She hasn't said anything.

MICK: Then why are we so abnormal?

MONICA: Not abnormal –

MICK: What do we do that's abnormal?

MONICA: Nothing. Please let's forget this –

MICK: You must think that for a reason.

MONICA: No, I don't.

MICK: You must.

MONICA: I suppose it's not strictly normal to… Please.

MICK: What?

MONICA: Let's forget this –

MICK: Not strictly normal to what?

MONICA: Not strictly normal to force her to sit on your back like that.

MICK: When have I forced her to sit on my back?

MONICA: I don't know when –

MICK: When have I forced her to sit on my back?!

MONICA: Please –

MICK: I do not force her to sit on my back!!!

Long pause.

MONICA: I'm so sorry. Forget this. I was feeling so happy, my mouth and my brain… Would you like some more to drink?

MONICA pours more wine into a truck. Pause.

Did you see the local paper? Somebody found a human bone in a waste paper basket.

Pause.

Say something.

MICK: What do you think I am?

MONICA: Please don't be upset.

MICK: What do you think I am?

MONICA: I didn't mean anything, I don't think you're anything. Please can we forget this?

MICK: It's not my fault she's the way she is.

MONICA: I think you're a wonderful father.

MICK: I love her.

MONICA: I know you do, I know how much you love her.

MICK: What does that mean?

MONICA: Nothing.

MICK: Then what?

MONICA: What?

MICK: What do you think I am?

MONICA: I think you're a wonderful man! That's why I'm so happy to be… I just thought you might feel… Sometimes you can almost love someone too much, can't you? Emotions are so complicated –

MICK: I have never touched her.

MONICA: Jesus Christ, I know.

MICK: If that's what you mean.

MONICA: I know that, I know –

MICK: I have never touched her!

MONICA: Jesus Christ –

MICK: She is my baby, Monica! Her Mummy died and she is damaged we are both damaged!

MONICA: Yes –

MICK: Every bone of both of us I would never hurt her!!

MONICA: No I know –

MICK: I clean her sheets and cook her food I clean her sheets and cook her food and she needs me!!!

MONICA: Yes –

MICK: She needs me!!!

MONICA: Yes –

MICK: I have never touched her!!!

MICK covers his face with his arm. Long pause.

MONICA: It's okay.

Pause.

It's okay, don't cry.

Pause. MONICA strokes MICK's hair…

Please don't cry, have a drink.

Pause. MICK stands and walks towards the door.

Don't leave yet. Please Mick…

MICK leaves.

Scene 3

BEN and EMILY stand at the edge of a river.

BEN: Are you feeling better now?

EMILY: Yes thanks. I don't think Monica's gin's as strong as that.

BEN: Yeah. Perhaps she doesn't drink it neat.

EMILY: Oh right. I don't know. Doesn't the river run quickly at night?

BEN: Yeah, it's wonderful.

EMILY: And look at the swans. Aren't they evenly spaced?

Pause.

University must be good.

BEN: You think so?

EMILY: What, don't you like it?

BEN: I don't know really. It's probably just a matter of expectations, but I was hoping for a bit more… philosophy and debating and tradition and history.

EMILY: Isn't it like that then?

BEN: Not really. Most of my lectures are in a gymnasium.

EMILY: Really?

BEN: Yeah, and my tutor's only twenty-three. He's got a pierced eyebrow, a black hooded top and blond dreadlocks down to his shoulders.

EMILY: My God, I bet you're more clever than him.

BEN: I don't know about that, but –

EMILY: I bet you are. You explain things better than anyone.

BEN: Me? It's you that said that the opposite of love was indifference.

Pause.

Listen, don't answer if you don't want, but…who were you speaking to earlier?

EMILY: She was at my school.

BEN: No, when I came back from the toilet. You were on your own but speaking. I was wondering who –

EMILY: Nobody.

BEN: Don't worry, nobody else saw you. I was just curious because –

EMILY: I wasn't speaking to anybody.

BEN: Sorry I… Forget it. Sorry.

Pause.

EMILY: Do you really want to know?

BEN: If you want to tell me.

EMILY: Can I tell you this?

BEN: Tell me what?

EMILY: I want to tell you something.

BEN: Tell me whatever you like.

EMILY: You'll probably think I'm a total… Anyway, I speak to my mum. I was speaking to my mum.

BEN: Oh right.

EMILY: I speak to my mum.

BEN: Okay. I don't know anything about your mum.

EMILY: She's not alive. She died four years ago.

BEN: My goodness, I didn't know that.

EMILY: Yeah, she died. She dived off a rock into very shallow water and broke her neck right through. And her spine right through. She was only very partially sighted.

BEN: That's really awful.

EMILY: Just colours and shapes.

BEN: That's terrible. Who told her it was safe?

EMILY: I did.

BEN: Sorry.

EMILY: I thought it was safe.

BEN: My God, that must feel really strange.

EMILY: It's why Dad wanted to leave the seaside. You only have to hold a shell to his ear and he starts crying.

Pause.

But anyway, yeah, she comes to me and I speak to her. I know it sounds idiotic.

BEN: It doesn't at all.

EMILY: I just try to make things better and apologise for what I did. And I try to make her…smile at me. This sounds so stupid.

BEN: It doesn't.

EMILY: But anyway, she doesn't forgive me. However much I apologise, she doesn't forgive me. She sometimes makes me think she has but she hasn't. She hasn't because then she hurts me. Cuts me or pulls my hair. I've got scars and everything.

BEN: Sorry... How does she do that?

EMILY: It isn't really her that does it, it's me. I pretend that it's her but really it's me. I do it to myself.

BEN: My goodness.

EMILY: The way she looks at me –

BEN: My goodness. Have you told your Dad or...Monica?

EMILY: I tell them I have bad dreams but none of this. You're the only person.

Pause.

BEN: It's difficult to know what to say. You really mustn't do that.

EMILY: I know.

BEN: You really mustn't.

EMILY: I have to apologise to her somehow.

BEN: I can see that but –

EMILY: It wouldn't be so bad if we still lived by the sea.

BEN: Wouldn't it?

EMILY: We'd be closer. She wouldn't think I'd run away from what I did. I could apologise into the sea. The sea would be there and I could.... It sounds idiotic when I say it out loud. You must think I'm mental.

BEN: That's okay. I don't think that.

Pause.

Listen, we might not live by the sea, but I think you can still…apologise into the sea. In a way. I mean, this river flows down to the sea.

Short pause.

What I mean is…you could send messages down the river to the sea. Rather than hurting yourself like that.

EMILY: What kind of messages?

BEN: Written messages saying sorry.

EMILY: That's not the same.

BEN: I know that, but it could be almost the same. Because you know the trick I taught you? The trick with the paper that goes up the string? That's how I speak to my Dad now he's gone.

EMILY: Really?

BEN: Yeah. If I'm feeling angry or missing him, I just make a kite and write a message. Then I go up the hills, fly the kite and send the message up the string. And then, when I feel ready, I let go of the kite. I watch it fly away.

EMILY: Isn't that a real waste of kites?

BEN: Not really. It makes me feel better.

Pause.

EMILY: What, so I just write out messages and throw them in the river?

BEN: You could.

EMILY: I'd look like a bit of an idiot.

BEN: So what, it's better than hurting yourself.

EMILY: What if she came to me anyway?

BEN: She won't though, will she? Not if you tell yourself she doesn't need to.

Pause.

EMILY: Okay…

BEN: Sorry, I don't mean to pressurise you –

EMILY: No, I will, I'll really try. Thanks.

Long pause.

BEN: It's amazing. I get this really awestruck feeling looking at the river. I suppose it's different if you've lived here a while.

EMILY: I've only ever seen it with my Dad in the daytime. It's better at night with you.

BEN: I can be really negative sometimes. I look at the world and the ozone layer and religion and wars and so many people… I panic that we'll run out of air or blow ourselves up or the earth will just open and swallow us in. Do you ever get those feelings?

EMILY smiles nervously.

But then you look at a river and the future seems a bit more certain, doesn't it? Look at your face.

EMILY: What?

BEN: Really frightened and sweet.

Pause.

But it also gives me this awestruck feeling where I hardly even know that I exist. The size of the river makes me feel so miniscule, I hardly feel like I exist at all. Like I need someone to touch me, just to let me know that I exist at all. Do you ever get those feelings?

EMILY: Yeah, I get exactly that.

BEN looks out down the river and EMILY looks at her hands. She moves a hand across to BEN's groin and begins to fondle.

BEN: Emily, stop it.

She continues. He moves away.

Stop it! Get off! What's the matter with you?

EMILY: What?

BEN: Just… What are you doing?! Why would you do that?!

EMILY: Because you said.

BEN: What? Said what?

EMILY: Touching.

BEN: Jesus Christ! I was speaking philosophically! About rivers! I didn't mean squeeze my balls! Why would you do that?

EMILY: I thought you wanted it. You said touching –

BEN: For God's sake, you're still a child!

Pause.

Emily, I'm sorry. Come on, I'm sorry.

EMILY: I want to go home now.

BEN: Don't be upset.

EMILY: I want to go home now!

BEN: Emily, please. Come on, please. I just got a bit of a shock. I over-reacted. Just unexpected. A misunderstanding, that's all. My fault.

He takes her hand.

Come on, you're shivering.

EMILY: You hate me now.

BEN: Of course I don't.

EMILY: You think I'm dirty.

He takes her other hand.

BEN: Of course I don't. I think you're really…innocent and beautiful.

He kisses her gently.

You look really pretty with tears all down your face.

They kiss again.

Scene 4

Morning in MONICA's shop. EMILY is sitting on a chair in the middle of the floor. MONICA stands behind EMILY, combing nits from her damp hair and cleaning the comb in a bowl of water. There is a notebook on the counter.

EMILY: Uh!!! The whole thing was a complete dream from start to finish! You should have seen it. He held me tight against his chest so I could hardly even breathe and he said that I should never be afraid, I should never give up and I should never apologise for what I am because what I am is beautiful and intriguing. Has a man ever said anything like that to you?

MONICA: No.

EMILY: And you're forty-six! Then what he did…

EMILY stands up to re-enact.

He lifted my chin up with his knuckle really gently, ran his finger down my collar bone, rubbed my nose with his while he sort of tickled my neck, then kissed my left eye, then kissed my right eye, then lifted me up to stand on his toes and kissed me really hard but really soft on the lips.

MONICA: It sounds like he knows what he's doing.

EMILY flounces away from the chair…

EMILY: He knows exactly what he's doing. I had no idea there were so many ways to kiss! He moves his tongue in these perfect little circles –

MONICA: Emily!

EMILY: In my mouth!

MONICA: I should hope in your mouth.

EMILY: Jesus Christ, we only kissed! What do you think I am?

MONICA moves the chair to where EMILY now stands.

But what a god of kissing!

EMILY sits on the chair.

A week until I see him again! I will explode before then! If he had seen that I had nits I think I would have dropped down dead.

MONICA: I've told you they go for the cleanest people.

EMILY: Monica, if you lined up everyone from my school that ever caught nits, you would not get the cleanest people. Believe me, you would get all the absolute dirtiest. What a humiliation!

MONICA: Please don't shout, my head is throbbing.

EMILY: I cannot believe I have him all to myself! He says he likes the lump where my collar bone broke! And he did this thing where he wrote this thing on a tiny piece of paper and he said I couldn't read it until some day in the future when I'm really really really really sad. Isn't that good?

MONICA: Lovely. Yes.

EMILY: And guess what it said.

MONICA: You read it?

EMILY: Of course I read it. It said 'Life is a rehearsal.' Isn't that the most amazing thing?

MONICA: Yes, it's –

EMILY: No sorry, 'Life is not a rehearsal.' Isn't that the most amazing thing? Because Ben says the single most biggest cause of unhappiness in the world is people's inability to grab at things. He says that everyone wants everything too perfect because of…fast food and the Internet. He says that people wish for things, but then when they come along they don't grab them because they have the wrong colour wrapping paper.

MONICA: Is that what he said?

EMILY: Yeah. I don't exactly know what he means, but I think he's probably right, don't you? And oh my God! You have to read his poems! They're about love and depression and there's one about homeless people. And he said this beautiful thing about rivers which I didn't understand at first, but I did when he said it again –

MONICA: Sorry Emily, I think I'll just get some fresh air. Feel a bit sick.

EMILY: Hang on, what about my hair?

MONICA: Just rinse it through in a minute or two.

EMILY: Yeah but Monica –

MONICA: I'll only be a minute.

PHIL PORTER

MONICA leaves the shop. EMILY sits for a moment, then stands up and pirouettes. She picks up the bowl of nits and water and carries it into the flat. She sings an arpeggio badly. She comes back into the shop and tidies in a balletic way while continuing to sing badly. There is a knock at the door.

EMILY: We're not open yet. Staff training.

MICK: (*Off.*) It's me.

EMILY: Oh. It's you.

EMILY unlocks the door and stands back.

Come on, then. It's open.

MICK comes in.

What do you want?

MICK: I saw Monica leave –

EMILY: What were you doing? Spying on the shop?

MICK: No, I was sitting in the park. When's she coming back?

EMILY: You should be careful. People will think you're a weirdo, sitting in parks.

MICK: Please…

Pause.

I'm really sorry, love –

EMILY: I had a lovely night thank you very much. I thought about spending the night in the bathroom, like you suggested, but then I thought I might have more fun with my boyfriend. You seem to forget that windows exist.

MICK: Will you let me explain?

EMILY: I haven't told Monica if that's what you're worried about.

MICK: I don't care about Monica, I want to explain.

EMILY: Why should I?

MICK: Because what happened –

EMILY: I know what happened, I was there.

MICK: Yes but I –

EMILY: Why should I listen to you?

MICK: Because I am trying to say sorry!

EMILY: Sounds like it.

MICK: I didn't mean to raise my voice. I've been awake all night –

EMILY: Really? Then who was that stinking drunk sprawled out on the carpet when I got back? And while we're at it, you wore those clothes yesterday. You stink. But yes, I had a lovely night. I got to do all sorts of things I've never done before.

Short pause.

Go on then. Ask me what we did. Ask what sexual things we did. That's why you're here.

MICK: That's not why I'm here.

EMILY: Of course it isn't.

MICK: I don't want to know.

EMILY: Of course you don't. You're so transparent, it's disgraceful. But as you are so desperate to know, I can tell you now that we did do quite a lot of very good kissing.

MICK: Stop that.

EMILY: In fact we kissed and kissed and kissed –

MICK: That's enough now.

EMILY: Or what? Kick me out if you like, I'll go and live with Ben.

MICK: I don't want to kick you out.

EMILY: I can also tell you that he liked my new underwear more than you did. Although I think he preferred the knickers to the bra. Especially when he pulled them off.

EMILY grabs the notebook and runs out.

MONICA: (*Off.*) Emily…?

MONICA comes in and sees MICK.

Oh…

MICK: I'll go.

MONICA: Don't go.

MICK: I'll leave you alone.

MONICA: No please don't go. I've got your coat. Please…

MONICA takes MICK's coat from a hiding place.

Please forgive me. I should never have said what I said. Can you forgive me?

MICK says nothing.

I've been so lonely, and when you said you needed me… I want so much to make things work between us. Have I wasted my chance?

MICK says nothing.

I haven't wasted my chance, have I?

MICK: I suppose not.

MONICA: Thank you.

MONICA gives MICK his coat back and nervously holds him. Long pause.

I just imagine the three of us. I think things are going to be wonderful.

Scene 5

BEN is by the river reading 'La Symphonie Pastorale'. EMILY appears, clutching a small wrapped present. It is early evening.

EMILY: I am so sorry.

BEN: That's okay.

EMILY: Please don't hate me for being late. A man on the bus was sick in his cap and it splashed a lady. Honestly, I have so much to tell you. This last week has seemed like months. Are you okay?

BEN: Yeah, listen –

EMILY: Aren't you even curious that I'm holding a wrapped-up present?

BEN: Sorry, who's that for?

EMILY: Can't you even guess? Stupid donkey, it's for you.

She gives him the present and he unwraps it.

You better like it. There's only one of them in the world.

It is a silver fountain pen.

BEN: My goodness, it's lovely.

EMILY: Think of the poems you'll write with that. Monica paid eighty pounds for it, then when I said you'd like it, she gave it me for free to give to you. Isn't that the loveliest thing? My dad's being lovely too, in a strange sort of way –

BEN: That's a lot of money –

EMILY: But do you want to know the really amazing thing? I did what you said and it worked. I've stopped. I've written a message every day and put it in the river here. Not once has she come to me and hurt me.

BEN: That's really good –

EMILY: I can still feel her with me, I can feel it in my face, but she just feels so much…more gentle. So yeah, the pen's to say thank you. And this as well…

EMILY tries to kiss BEN. He backs away.

BEN: No, I didn't come for that. I really didn't come for that.

EMILY: I did.

She tries again and he backs away again.

BEN: No please, let me speak. There's something… Let me think…

Pause. BEN scratches his head.

Do you have lice in your hair?

EMILY: No.

BEN: My head's been itching ever since we went out.

EMILY: I don't even know what they look like.

BEN: That's fine, I just –

EMILY: Check my head if you like. Check it, it's as clean as anything.

BEN: No that's fine. Honestly, I believe you.

EMILY: Good.

EMILY takes BEN's hand. Short pause.

BEN: That's not what I wanted to say. What I wanted to say… I wanted to apologise.

EMILY: What for?

BEN takes his hand away.

BEN: Everything. The going out and the being nice. The kissing. I hope I didn't give the impression that it might happen again.

Short pause.

EMILY: Are you dumping me?

BEN: You are such a good person.

EMILY: Are you dumping me because I gave you nits?

BEN: I'm not dumping you, I was never your boyfriend. Listen, you are such a good, such a sweet person and I really want you to be happy but… I was just trying to be a comfort. After you grabbed me like that, you looked so upset. I got confused, I thought I was helping. I honestly never imagined you'd want to do it again and buy me things.

EMILY: Monica bought it.

BEN: I can't take it.

BEN gives the pen back. Pause.

And I want to be totally honest with you. I have a new girlfriend now. A girl from college called Olivia. We have things in common. We like the same authors, it's wonderful. I was hoping that you might be happy for me.

EMILY: No.

BEN: It's so difficult. You're ever so young.

EMILY: You're only nineteen!

BEN: I know that.

EMILY: You're not the king!

BEN: I know that but… I just want to make things easy. I really don't know what to say. It's a matter of compatibility.

BEN starts leafing through his book.

I read something in this book that I thought was so true. It's called 'La Symphonie Pastorale' –

EMILY throws the book on the ground.

Emily!

EMILY: I told everyone! You said I was intriguing!

BEN: I did say that. You are intriguing.

EMILY: You said I was beautiful!

BEN: I know I said that.

EMILY: Then why didn't you mean it?!

BEN picks up his book.

How can you kill me like this? How can you kiss me on the eyes and not mean it?

BEN: I deserve for you to throw my book.

EMILY: You deserve to be shot.

BEN: Listen, I've done something wrong. I've upset you, I've made you feel stupid, I'm sorry but… For God's sake, people kiss all the time.

EMILY: Not like they love each other.

BEN: We hardly know each other!

EMILY looks away. Pause.

I think you're incredible, Emily. You seem to be walking on such a tightrope. Your life seems to be balanced on the apex of everything and that's wonderful.

Pause.

Actually, the apex thing was Olivia's idea. She says you sound like such a lovely girl.

Pause.

Would you like me to take you home?

EMILY: Go away.

BEN: I can go away if you want me to.

EMILY: I hate you I could kill you I could kill you I could.

BEN: You don't mean that.

EMILY: Go away I said!

BEN wipes down the cover of his book.

Go away go away go away before I kill you!! Get lost before I kill you!!!

BEN: Okay –

EMILY: Leave me alone!!!

BEN leaves. EMILY takes the pen from its box. The sound of the sea creeps in.

He didn't even see, Mummy. He didn't even see what I had engraved.

Scene 6

MONICA's shop. MONICA is sitting on a chair. MICK kneels in front of MONICA, between her legs, applying make-up to her face with a brush. There is a bottle of gin on the counter.

MONICA: You don't mind doing this?

MICK says nothing.

Every nerve and skin cell waking up from ten years sleep. Little waves across my skin. Can you imagine the three of us living by the sea?

MICK: I don't want to live by the sea.

MONICA: Perhaps we should go on holiday, the three of us, she'd like that. Once we've told her. Sorry, I just can't wait until everything's…

Long pause. MONICA nervously kisses MICK.

I painted my bedroom this week. Would you like to come through to my bedroom?

Short pause.

Stay there, I'll call you through in a moment. I'll light some candles. Nicer with candles…

MONICA goes. MICK goes to the counter and drinks gin from the bottle. MONICA appears at the doorway.

Forgot the matches.

MONICA takes matches into the flat. Pause. EMILY comes into the shop. Her face is wet with tears and one of her arms is punctured and covered in blood and ink.

EMILY: He doesn't want me, Daddy.

MICK: Jesus Christ. Emily –

EMILY: He says I'm not compatible. He says I'm on the apex of everything. What does that mean?

MICK: Emily, your arm.

EMILY: I hate him so much.

MICK: What have you done to your arm?

EMILY looks at her arm. He tries to usher her out.

Let's go home, let's get you home.

EMILY: Where's Monica?

MICK: You'll get blood on the floor –

EMILY: Where's Monica? What are you doing here?

MICK: Nothing. Come on, I'll take you home –

MONICA: (*Off.*) You can come through…

EMILY: Who's she talking to?

MICK: Nobody.

EMILY: What does she mean?

MICK: Nothing, let's get out –

MONICA appears in the doorway…

MONICA: What's all the shouting?

Pause.

EMILY: What's happening.?

MICK: She's not very well. I dropped by, she was sick on the floor, I told her to go to bed. Go back to bed, Monica.

Short pause.

Go back to bed, Monica. Let's leave Monica to get some rest.

EMILY: Dad?

MICK: Don't you look at me like that. I told you she was sick on the floor! Go back to bed, Monica!

EMILY: He's done your make-up, he's done your eyes…

MONICA: Emily, we have some news that we're excited about and we hope that you will be too.

EMILY: No…

MONICA: Me and your dad, we really like each other very much and we believe that there's a future. Don't be upset.

EMILY: I'm thinking.

MONICA: What are you thinking?

EMILY: I'm thinking it's disgusting. I'm wondering whether to puke. I'm wondering why people bother pretending to like me.

MONICA: Don't say that.

EMILY: I'll say what I want. You're a pair of bare-faced fucking liars. You're a dirty old man and a stinking dirty prostitute.

MONICA: Emily, please –

EMILY: You're a pair of perverted fucking dogs that stink of piss.

MONICA: Oh my God, your arm!

MONICA takes EMILY's arm.

Emily, what have you done to yourself?

EMILY: Don't touch me.

MONICA: Emily, what on earth…?!

EMILY: Don't you fucking touch me!!!

MICK: Stop swearing!!!

EMILY: Or what, you liar, you fucking liar?

MICK: I am telling you...

EMILY: Murder me, I don't care. Grab my ankles and smash me against the wall. You promised me.

MICK: I never promised anything.

EMILY: I told you I would die if this ever happened. I pray every night that this won't happen.

MICK: Don't be so stupid.

EMILY: Why does no-one ever fucking listen to what I'm saying?! Why does nothing ever fucking happen like I want it?!

MICK: You get what you deserve.

EMILY: I don't deserve to be stabbed in the face!!

MONICA: She needs to go to hospital.

MICK: It's not my fault he doesn't want you.

EMILY: It is your fault! It's you that brought me up like a baby! It's you that made me weird!

MICK: I have cared for you!

EMILY: You're fucking cruel is what you are! You hate me!

MICK: I have loved you!

EMILY: You don't know what it means, you liar, you fucking liar, I hate you! I wish you were dead, dead, dead in a hole in the ground! I wish your fucking neck would break! I wish you'd died as well as mum, I wish you'd died as well!!!

MICK grabs EMILY and forces her to the ground, face down...

MICK: You say that again.

EMILY: Get your hands off me.

MICK: Get on the floor!

MONICA: Mick. Stop. Stop it!!!

> *MONICA tries to intervene. MICK throws her off. EMILY spits at MICK. He pins her to the floor and starts smacking her bum. EMILY wails, thrashes and tries to break away.*

MICK: You say that again!

MONICA: Please stop –

MICK: Say it!

EMILY: I wish you were dead!

MICK: You spiteful girl.

EMILY: Stop fucking hitting me!

MICK: You vicious girl. You spiteful girl.

> *MONICA tries again to intervene but is pushed away.*

Stay out of it!

EMILY: You're hurting me!

MICK: You're lucky I'm not wringing your neck!

EMILY: Daddy please!!

MONICA: Stop it now!!!

MICK: I have loved you!!

EMILY: Daddy get off!!!

MICK: You are a disgrace to your mother!!

> *MICK suddenly stops smacking. He moves back from EMILY. She stands up, not taking her eyes off him. He looks ashamed.*

Silence. EMILY runs and throws herself at the free-standing unit of shelving, knocking it over and sending its contents crashing across the shop.

Scene 7

It is late at night. MONICA is mending a vase. EMILY is sitting somewhere. Her arm is now bandaged. She is staring into the side of MONICA's head.

MONICA: Would you like to borrow one of my jumpers?

EMILY: No. I hate all of your jumpers.

Long pause.

MONICA: I saw the girl from the carpet shop earlier. She had a spot on her chin so big I thought it was a redcurrant. In fact, it's so big, I thought she had a Siamese twin.

EMILY: I hope it burst into your face. Your voice is like grinding metal.

MONICA: If that's the way you feel, why don't you go home and speak to your dad. Surely that would be more interesting than staring into the side of my head.

Pause.

So my voice isn't so bad.

EMILY: No, your voice is disgusting, just not quite as disgusting as him.

MONICA: He loves you.

EMILY: I don't need you to tell me that.

Pause.

He doesn't love you, if that's what you think. He told me he preferred the dog next door. No let me get this right, he said he preferred cheese and biscuits and that you were exactly the same as the dog next door. He wouldn't have gone near you if I hadn't upset him.

MONICA: I know that.

EMILY: Then you're even sadder than I thought. I suppose you've seen the picture of my mum by his bed.

Silence as MONICA continues mending the vase.

MONICA: Is your arm okay?

EMILY: Tetanus jab is the best thing that's happened to me today.

MONICA: Thank God there wasn't more ink in the wound.

Pause.

I never thought you'd take it quite that far.

EMILY: What do you mean?

MONICA: We're not blind. We have seen the little scabs and bruises.

EMILY: Then why didn't you say something?!

Pause.

You're such a pair of fuckers.

EMILY leaves the shop, taking a detour to topple the almost mended vase. It breaks on the floor.

Scene 8

The park. EMILY is sunbathing on the diving board. She is wearing a bikini and sunglasses and lying on a towel. Her arm is still bandaged and her body is bruised and scabbed. She is wearing a set of headphones that are not plugged into anything. MICK is laying out a blanket on the grass by the pool.

MICK: Come down now, it's dirty up there. Come down and sit on the blanket, I know they're not plugged in.

Pause.

Monica's made you a picnic, the least you can do is come down.

Pause.

I won't be made to feel guilty, Emily. I have no reason.

MICK sits on the blanket. Pause. MONICA arrives with a bag full of food.

MONICA: You don't mind if we join you, Emily? This bag's cutting into my hands. Would you like to come and join us on the blanket?

MONICA unpacks the picnic.

One punnet of peaches. Cheese triangle sandwiches on brown. Bread sticks, celery, taramasalata. Cold sausages. Cold baked beans. Chocolate. Apple juice. Water. Now is there enough blue sky to make a Dutchman's trousers? That's what I want to know.

MICK: Come and get some food.

Pause.

Come and get some food.

MONICA: I forgot to bring mustard.

EMILY: Isn't it funny how quick the fucking clouds come over?

Pause. MONICA prepares a plate of food for EMILY, the centrepiece of which is a peach, and places it on the diving board.

MONICA: You should have seen us this morning. Like a pair of silly monkeys, combing the nits from each other's hair.

MICK: She can get her own food.

MONICA: I don't mind.

Pause.

I had a hilarious phone call this morning. This will make both of you laugh.

Her audience is not so convinced.

What happened, a man phoned wanting to sell an engraved silver plate, okay? I think it was an engraved souvenir plate from the Silver Jubilee. Anyway, guess what his name was. Emily, guess what his name was. His name was Nicholas Graves. His name was N Graves. Isn't that a hilarious coincidence? So I asked him what his wife was called and if she was called M Broidery, which I thought was quite funny as well, but he said she was actually called Caroline Graves, which is C Graves. As in sea burial.

Short pause.

I often think I'd like to be buried at sea.

Long pause. EMILY starts unravelling the kite string.

Isn't it peaceful for a Sunday? Isn't it lovely?

EMILY: Please will you be quiet, Monica. You're making my fucking brain bleed.

MONICA: Are you going to fly the kite?

EMILY: No.

MONICA: Why don't you fly the kite?

MICK: She doesn't want to.

MONICA: Come on, fly the kite.

EMILY: I don't want to.

MONICA: I'd love to see you fly it though. He spent lots of money –

EMILY: It's not designed properly. It won't get any fucking lift.

MONICA: Don't be like this.

EMILY: Like fucking what?

MICK: She said she doesn't want to fly it.

MONICA: Just for a little while –

MICK: If she doesn't want to fly it, she doesn't have to!

Pause.

EMILY: There's a dead black beetle up here with a white bit on its back like a fucking skull and cross-bones.

MONICA: I think I'll fetch some mustard.

Pause. MONICA leaves. EMILY starts to wrap herself in the string from the kite, constricting her arms and legs. Silence.

MICK: Tell me what you want. Tell me what you want!

EMILY totters to the edge of the diving board.

Come back from there. Emily, stand back from there.

EMILY: The seaside.

MICK: What?

EMILY: I want to go to the seaside.

MICK: Okay, next weekend, come on, there's broken glass down there.

EMILY: To live.

MICK: Come away now.

EMILY: To live.

MICK: Talk about it later.

EMILY: Talk about it now.

MICK: No, get down now.

EMILY: I mean this, I'll do it, I'll jump. I'll jump and smash my cheekbones and I'll say that you pushed me. Seaside.

MICK: Okay, sit down here on the blanket and we'll talk.

EMILY: I don't want to talk.

MICK: Come down here, we'll talk, no pony's back.

EMILY begins to bounce on the end of the board.

EMILY: I swear, I'll crack my fucking cheekbones.

MICK: Emily, please.

EMILY: I'll smash my nose across my face.

MICK: Please, just stop.

EMILY: I'll break my wrists and ankles.

MICK: Emily, please, I'm sorry, please, I'm sorry…!

EMILY: Then say it.

MICK: I am sorry.

EMILY: Say we can go back.

MICK says nothing. She bounces higher.

Say we can go back!

Bouncing higher…

Say we can go back, Dad!!

Bouncing higher…

Say we can go back!!

MICK: We can go back.

EMILY: Say we can go back!!

MICK: We can go back!!

EMILY stops bouncing.

Let's go back to the seaside.

EMILY: You don't mean that.

MICK: Yes I do.

EMILY: You're just saying that.

MICK: No, we'll move back to the seaside.

EMILY: Really?

MICK: Yes.

EMILY: It's what I want.

MICK: I want it too.

MICK climbs onto the diving board. Pause.

EMILY: Can we leave today?

MICK: Okay.

EMILY: Come back for our things when we're settled.

MICK: Yeah.

EMILY: Can we buy our old house?

MICK: If you want.

EMILY: I want to build a house on the beach.

MICK puts his arms around EMILY.

I want to live at the seaside.

MICK: I know you do.

EMILY: Like before, just us, no Monica.

MICK: Just us.

EMILY: That's what I want.

End.

LATCHMERE

Starting life back in 1982 as the Gate Theatre at the Latchmere, a sister theatre to the Gate Theatre Notting Hill, one of London's best known studio theatres celebrated its twentieth anniversary in 2002.

'The Latchmere is a tiny theatre in Battersea – a David amidst the West End's sluggish Goliaths'
Observer, March 2003

Since April 2002 the Latchmere Theatre has been supporting new writing and encouraging new and emerging playwrights, such as Ursula Rani Sarma, Dennis Kelly, Glyn Cannon, Peter Morris, Ronan O'Donnell and Samantha Ellis, as well as staging new works by more established writers including Ron Hutchinson, Naomi Wallace and Fraser Grace.

'The Latchmere…consistently unearthing some of London theatre's most exciting new voices.'
Time Out, April 2003

Artistic Director	Paul Higgins
Associate Directors	Johnnie Lyne Pirkis
	Phil Hewitt
Associate Artist	Jenny MacDonald
Associates	Helen Neale, Anna Ledwich,
	Andrew Higgins, Cova Montes,
	Selina Papoutseli, Jamie Wood,
	Kirstie Miller, Kali Hughes,
	Bill Buckhurst, Nick Hayman-
	Joyce, Lorraine Cheesmur

www.latchmeretheatre.com

Stealing Sweets and Punching People was written and developed in conjunction with the National Theatre Studio